Greatest
MOMENTS OF
GRAND PRIX

This edition first published in the UK in 2007
By Green Umbrella Publishing

© Green Umbrella Publishing 2007

www.greenumbrella.co.uk

Publishers: Jules Gammond and Vanessa Gardner

Printed and bound in China

ISBN: 978-1-906229-41-2

Greatest
MOMENTS OF
GRAND PRIX

by JON STROUD

CONTENTS

CONTENTS

GERMAN GRAND PRIX – NÜRBURGRING
1957

Known locally as die Grüne Hölle – the Green Hell – the Nürburgring is a circuit like no other. Completed in the spring of 1927 its Nordschleife (Northern Loop) twists and turns around 100 bends for a treacherous 14 miles through Germany's Eifel mountains and has widely been regarded as the most testing motor racing circuit in the world.

The 1957 German Grand Prix was set to be an exciting affair. At 46 years old, Juan-Manuel Fangio had dominated the season by winning three of the previous four races and was set to take his fifth World Championship. Only an unfortunate engine failure at the British Grand Prix which had allowed the Vanwall of Stirling Moss to take victory had prevented him from maintaining a perfect record. Demonstrating the supremacy for which he had become known, qualification was a mere formality with his 9:25.6 placing his Alfa Romeo 250F almost three seconds clear of the second-placed Ferrari of Mike Hawthorn. Two seconds further in arrears was the Maserati of Frenchman Jean Behra whilst Peter Collins' Ferrari languished yet further behind in fourth having qualified over nine seconds down of the Argentinean ace.

For all the skill of their drivers, the premier teams knew that their race strategy would be critical for success. As race day dawned and a blazing sun filled the cloudless sky it was clear that tyre wear would be the deciding factor. After assessing the situation the Maserati team decided that they would bring their cars in at half distance for fresh rubber thus allowing them to start the race with a half load of fuel, saving precious weight on the rolling mountain circuit. Ferrari, on the other hand, elected to run their race non-stop; this would mean that their tyres would have to be conserved but time would not be wasted in the pit lane. After all, a few seconds lost in a Grand Prix can present an insurmountable challenge to even the best driver.

As the starter dropped his flag it was the Ferrari team who were first to take the advantage – Mike Hawthorn powering into the lead as the cars set off on their first circuit followed closely by his team mate Peter Collins. It was not long, however, before Fangio, taking full advantage of his Maserati's reduced weight, made his move. Breezing past on the third lap he was then able to

push steadily on until the need for fuel and fresh tyres forced him into the pits at the end of his 12th lap.

As he sped into the pit lane it seemed as if the Maserati tactics were going to pay dividends. He already had a 28-second lead and could feasibly join the fray level with his Maranello rivals but with the advantage of fresh tyres. But the best laid plans can come to nought in the wink of an eye. Whether influenced by the occasion or affected by the searing heat, the Maserati team's pit stop was appalling. Fangio could do nothing but wait as his mechanics fumbled with wheels and fuel lines and desperately tried to reattach the maestro's seat which had broken away as the car was jostled over the harsh mountain roads.

With his foot hard to the floor Fangio screamed his way out of the pits and back onto the circuit but all his good work of the first 170 miles had been undone. In the first half of the race with the advantage of a lighter fuel load he had managed to pull 28 seconds clear but now, although running with fresh tyres, the fuel loads would be about equal and what was more he was now 80 seconds adrift. The pit stop had taken almost two minutes!

Timing the cars as they passed it seemed as if Ferrari's tactics had won the day. Not only was Fangio well behind but he was failing to make any impression on the progress of Hawthorn and Collins. Keen to let their drivers know that the pressure was off a message was displayed from the pits as the cars sped around for their 14th circuit. But the race was far from over; Fangio's lacklustre lap times following his pit stop were far from a signal of defeat. Always the master tactician, he was carefully allowing his tyres to warm up and bed in without subjecting them to excessive wear. The race was on!

As Fangio flew past the finish line to commence his 15th circuit panic erupted in the Ferrari pit. The Argentinean had broken the lap record! To make matters worse there was no way of informing the relaxed Hawthorn and Collins until they had completed their 14-mile lap. Even when they knew what was happening behind them there was nothing that the Ferraris could do to counter Fangio's assault. In what has been described as the most outstanding display of driving ever witnessed, each lap was completed in a new record time culminating in a staggering 9:17.4, eight seconds quicker than his pole qualifying time, as Collins and Hawthorn came into sight on the 20th tour. There was no stopping the Champion-in-waiting as he flew past both drivers over the Eifel Mountains and powered on to take his 24th final, and undoubtedly greatest, win of his career.

A GENTLEMAN'S CHAMPIONSHIP
1958

The lacklustre start of the 1958 world championship gave little indication of the drama, controversy and excitement that were to be in store as the year progressed. Nor did it hint at the down-to-the-wire finale or unparalleled sportsmanship that would hand one man the world title and rob the other of his best ever chance of taking motor racing's crown.

The opening round of the competition in Buenos Aires saw little support from many of the major teams. Ferrari sent three of their new Dino 246s for works drivers Mike Hawthorn, Peter Collins and Luigi Musso but Maserati, although well represented with six cars on the grid, were not themselves present having decided at the end of the previous year to withdraw from racing due to financial difficulties. The only other car present was the Cooper-Climax T43 of Stirling Moss who, with his new Vanwall unready for competition, had been temporarily released from his contract to enable him to take to the start line.

This was to prove a stroke of luck for the Briton and the Cooper team. Electing to drive the full distance without pitting for tyres or fuel, Moss stormed home to victory ahead of Musso and Hawthorn, and in doing so scored the first ever victory for the Cooper Car Company and the first for a post-war rear-engined car.

As the championship moved to Monaco the previously dominant Ferraris were once more denied victory as, for a second time, victory went to a Cooper-Climax; this time in the hands of Frenchman Maurice Trintignant. Unfortunately for Moss he had been forced to retire whilst leading when, after 38 laps, the engine of his new Vanwall failed. Hawthorn immediately took over the running in the Ferrari but he too suffered mechanical difficulties with a broken fuel pump and was back in his garage just 10 laps later.

Things went considerably better for Moss at the third round held at Zandvoort in the Netherlands. Although out-qualified by his Vanwall team mate, Stuart Lewis-Evans, Moss led from the first corner to the finish line to take an unquestionable victory in complete style. With the BRMs of Harry Schell and Jean Behra taking second and third and a Cooper-Climax driven by Roy

Salvadori securing fourth, it was another dry weekend for Ferrari; their best placed machine being that of Hawthorn back in fifth.

The Belgian Grand Prix was another success story for the Vanwall team. This time it was Tony Brooks who took victory honours with Lewis-Evans in third with the pair split by the Ferrari of Hawthorn. Moss, victim to another bout of bad luck, had missed a gear change on the first lap of the race and blown his engine in spectacular fashion.

Three weeks later and the teams were back in action once more – this time at the French Grand Prix. With Hawthorn in pole position ahead of Moss and the Ferraris of Wolfgang von Trips and Peter Collins in third and fifth split by the Maserati of Juan-Manuel Fangio, who was racing in his last ever Grand Prix, it was apparent that the Prancing Horse was back on form. Replicating the superb drive of his rival in Holland, Hawthorn held his lead from the start and was never once challenged on his way to taking victory almost 25 seconds ahead of second-placed Moss.

Ferrari was able to maintain this new found momentum as the racing moved to Britain and the Silverstone circuit. On this occasion it was Collins who took victory ahead of his team mate Hawthorn and the Cooper of Salvadori. Moss, meanwhile, was once again a victim of the Vanwall's fragile engine having covered only one third of the distance before going out with mechanical problems. Neither Hawthorn nor Moss could score points on the Nürburgring a fortnight later as both were again victims to mechanical failure. However, both were considerably more fortunate than Hawthorn's team mate Collins who was tragically killed when his Ferrari somersaulted after running wide and hitting a ditch.

The following round at an atypically wet Oporto street circuit in Portugal was to become the defining moment of the season. Having qualified in pole position Moss was quick to take command of the racing order but, as the cars struggled for grip on tramlines and cobbles, it was Hawthorn who soon moved into the lead on lap 2. Regaining control Moss retook the lead six laps later and continued to dominate for the remainder of the race to take victory ahead of his countryman and rival. But it was soon reported that Hawthorn had infringed the rules by pushing his Ferrari the wrong way after a spin and was, therefore, disqualified. First to protest was Moss. In his characteristically polite but firm manner he pointed out that when Hawthorn had pushed his car it was actually on the pavement and, therefore, no offence had taken place. After considering the plea of the winning driver it was decided to reinstate Hawthorn allowing the original result to stand.

This was to have a dramatic effect as the championship moved into its final round at the Ain-Diab circuit in Morocco. With Hawthorn having placed second during the penultimate round at Monza with Moss once again failing to finish, the championship was down to the wire. Moss knew that he not only had to win but also set the fastest lap of the race to gain an extra point and even this would only secure the championship if Hawthorn finished in third place or below. Moss drove the race of his life – first securing pole then setting the fastest lap and ultimately taking an emphatic victory by almost 85 seconds – but it was Hawthorn who had taken second place and subsequently the title by a single point.

Hawthorn was celebrated as the first English world champion but it would have been a different story had the gentlemanly and sporting conduct of Stirling Moss not handed him the six points that had secured him overall victory. Sadly Hawthorn's victory was to be short lived when, just three months later, he was killed having lost control of his Jaguar road car on the Guildford by-pass in Surrey.

MONACO GRAND PRIX 1961

The 1961 season marked another change to the Formula regulations that governed the world championship. Gone were the 2.5 litre cars of previous years and in their place a new breed of smaller, lighter 1.5 litre racers in an attempt to reduce speeds, increase safety and encourage more manufacturers to enter the championship with the prospect of lower development and running costs.

Despite an all-new grid there was no doubt in the minds of the sport's followers who the outstanding favourites for the championship were – Ferrari! Their new Carlo Chiti-designed shark-nosed Dino156, one of the most beautiful and distinctive cars ever to grace Formula 1, was fitted with the company's Type 178 V6 motor; an engine that had already benefited from over a year of testing and development in the hands of the Maranello engineers. It was also clear that the team had the talent to capitalise on their automotive supremacy. American Richie Ginther, competing in only his second season, had already scored a second place in the Italian Grand Prix at Monza the previous year whilst his countryman and more experienced team mate Phil Hill had seven podium finishes and a win to his name. In the third Scuderia Ferrari 156 was Count Wolfgang von Trips, a veteran of more than 20 Grand Prix starts and no stranger to the glory of the winner's podium. There was, however, one man who was determined to upset the rosso applecart – Stirling Moss, driving a new Lotus-Climax 18 for the privateer Rob Walker Racing Team.

Competition was so close that qualification saw the first eight places on the grid separated by less than a single second but it was Moss who, with an outstanding 1:39.1 for the 1.95 mile circuit, had placed himself in pole position ahead of the Ferrari of Ginther, the factory Lotus of Scotsman Jim Clark and the BRM of Graham Hill. Clark's time was set despite him having crashed heavily during the session; a fate which also befell his Lotus team mate Innes Ireland who was badly injured after being thrown from his car.

As the sun beat down on the hot sticky tarmac the cars lined up for the start of the XIX Grand Prix de Monaco. In an attempt to make for a more comfortable ride and with aerodynamics being less important on the twisting street circuit, Moss had decided to run with the side panels of his

Lotus-Climax removed making for an unusual and exciting view for the 30,000 spectators that packed the street corners, bars and rooftops.

As the starter's flag dropped it was Ginther who immediately took the advantage making good use of his Ferrari's additional 30bhp and lighter weight to make the first corner ahead of Moss. As the cars completed the first lap Ginther held Moss who was himself pursued by the fast moving Porsche 718s of Bonnier and Hermman in the first ever Grand Prix outing for the German marque. A lap later Ginther had extended his lead to five seconds but for Moss it was a case of playing a waiting game. He knew that he needed to spend time watching and observing his young rival if he was going to attack and stay clear.

With 13 corners and 90 gear shifts per lap the Monaco Grand Prix is always hard on cars and it was the BRM of Graham Hill that was first to fall by the wayside when its fuel pump failed on lap 11. Then, just three laps later, Moss picked his time to strike; forcing a heavy move on the approach to Casino he pushed his way into the lead whilst, in the confusion, Bonnier capitalised on the situation to also pass Ginther and take second. For Ferrari things were not looking good so it came as a relief when, with wheels almost touching, Phil Hill scraped past both his team mate and the silver Porsche to put his shark-nose Dino into second. The chase was on!

Lap after lap was set at speeds well above those managed by the old 2.5 litre cars that had been deemed too fast in the previous season but the Ferrari could do nothing to reel in Moss who was driving the inch-perfect race of his life. Ginther again found himself in third as Bonnier was soon left to watch from the sidelines when his Porsche coughed and spluttered to a halt on lap 39 with a fuel injection pump failure. Now it was Ginther who was setting the pace, his Dino soon closing the gap to his Ferrari team mate as Hill suffered from fading brakes.

On lap 73 the Ferrari pit signalled their cars – Ginther was to pass Hill and try to catch the Englishman – and with a wave of the hand he was through and hunting down Moss. The gap was closed to within 10 seconds and then to five but every time the American tried to apply the pressure the quiet and confident Moss had more than enough to respond.

After 195 miles and 100 laps of racing his job was done. Ferrari may have managed to place their cars in second, third and fourth places despite Von Trips crashing on his last lap but, by crossing the line just 3.6 seconds ahead of Ginther's Ferrari in an underpowered Lotus, the Englishman had taken the greatest victory of his life and in doing so shown up the most prestigious racing marque in the world.

ITALIAN GRAND PRIX – MONZA
1965

It is not uncommon in the world of Formula 1 for a season to be completely dominated by a single driver. From Alberto Ascari's supremacy in 1952 to the recent phenomenon of Michael Schumacher there has often been one driver who stands head and shoulders above his contemporaries.

From the start of the 1965 season there was but one competitor worth speaking about. Lotus driver Jim Clark had started and won six of the first seven championship rounds with four pole positions to his name. The only trophy thus far that failed to bear his name was that of the Monaco Grand Prix for which he was a non-starter, having elected to travel across the Atlantic to compete in the Indianapolis 500; a race which he had won in great style. With non-championship victories at Syracuse and Goodwood it was without a doubt a golden year for the farmer from Fife.

As the teams and drivers moved on to the Monza track for the Italian Grand Prix it appeared to be business as usual. At the close of a frantic and charged qualifying session it was once again Clark who headed the tables with only John Surtees in his Ferrari and Jackie Stewart in a BRM able to stay within one second of his time to join him on the front row of the grid. Filling the second row was a second BRM driven by Graham Hill, the Ferrari of Lorenzo Bandini and the Honda RA272 of Californian Ronnie Bucknam.

On race day, Italian hopes of seeing a Ferrari take the lead from the start were dashed as soon as the race director dropped his flag when Surtees' machine, suffering from an enormous degree of clutch slip, immediately dropped back to 14th place whilst Clark, displaying the grim determination and tenacity for which he had become known, catapulted his Lotus into the lead closely pursued by Stewart, Hill and Bandini. For the excited Italian spectators on that warm and sunny September afternoon it was nearly impossible to keep up with the action as the lead cars traded places almost on a lap by lap basis. Clark's lead was usurped on lap three only for him to take it back one circuit of the track later. But then Stewart took control, passing both his BRM team mate and the Lotus – then Clark again, then Stewart and then, to the surprise and delight of the countless Tifosi lining the banks and grandstands it was the gleaming red Ferrari of John Surtees

that slipped into the lead having driven clean through the field minus a clutch to take command of proceedings.

As the race progressed so the running order continued to change as Clark, Stewart, Surtees and Hill battled with hammer and tongs for supremacy. Eventually the frenetic pace paid its toll on Surtees' ailing Ferrari and with gears crunching and the smell of burning clutch plates he eventually drifted back through the field until retiring at the end of his 34th lap.

By the time the race had reached half distance the lead had changed hands 22 times but still Clark, Hill and Stewart fought with a passion rarely seen on the race track. Any semblance of tactics seemed to have been completely thrown out of the window as the three continued to trade places as they carved their way through countless backmarkers. With the race entering its closing stages and all three frontrunners posting inseparable lap times it was impossible to pick a winner. Having driven with unparalleled precision for the best part of the season, it would have taken a brave man to bet against Clark but, in the best tradition of Formula 1, the race is never over until the drivers cross the finish line at the end of the final lap.

Unfortunately for Clark on this occasion the final lap was never to be seen. Having duelled with the BRMs for 63 laps his perfect season came to an end with an undignified sputter as his engine gasped for fuel, its pump broken in a rare display of unreliability for the Lotus.

Hill and Stewart continued to fight as the laps counted down one by one; each taking their turn at the front with clockwork regularity. Then, with just three laps remaining, Hill took the bit between his teeth and started to charge for home. Driving at an incredible pace but with brutally defensive lines it looked to all as if the race was sewn up in favour of the Englishman but with little more than a lap to go it all went wrong. Carrying too much speed into the notorious Parabolica he drifted off line and started to slide. With lightning reactions he corrected himself within a fraction of a second but it was too late. Stewart had seized the opportunity, slipped through into first place and was now powering away towards the finish. It was the 43rd time in 76 laps that the lead had changed hands!

When the young Scotsman took the chequered flag he also took his first of many Formula 1 victories, having only competed in eight world championship events. A star was born.

BRABHAM'S HOMEMADE CHAMPIONSHIP
1966

A significant change in the rules heralded the start of the 1966 Formula 1 World Championship. Since 1961 the maximum permitted capacity of the cars had been limited to just 1500cc but, in a landmark decision, the regulations had been amended to allow the use of engines up to 3.0 litres. Horsepower was back but, just as the move to the smaller capacity had caused chaos and consternation at the start of the 1961 season, so the new changes had thrown many of the manufacturers into turmoil as the first race approached.

Unwilling to develop a 3.0 litre engine, Coventry Climax had announced their withdrawal from competition whilst Lotus, their new Ford Cosworth engine still under development, were forced to use an older design from British manufacturer BRM. Ferrari, meanwhile, had elected to use a shimmed down version of their successful 3.3 litre V12 sportscar engine. Jack Brabham, world champion in 1959 and 1960 and owner of his own team, the Brabham Racing Organisation, chose to commission Repco, the Australian engineering firm with whom he shared their Surbiton premises, to produce an engine of his own based upon an obsolete V8 Oldsmobile production engine. This decision would prove to pay dividends as the season progressed.

The opening race at Monaco was a shambolic affair. Such was the lack of preparedness that even reigning champion Jim Clark was forced to drive a year-old car fitted with a 2.0 litre Climax engine, although this failed to prevent the superlative Scot from taking pole position from the Ferrari 312 of John Surtees with the BRMs of Hill and Stewart relegated to third and fourth. However, as the race started it was Surtees who surged ahead into the first corner making good use of his additional horsepower. Surtees continued to lead the procession until lap 16 when his transmission failed forcing him to retire. He was soon followed first by Brabham with gearbox problems and then by Spence, Rindt and Clark as one by one the hard twisting nature of the course got the better of the poorly tested machinery. By the time Jackie Stewart's BRM victoriously crossed the finish line ahead of Bandini's Ferrari only six cars were still running and two of these, the Cooper-Maseratis of Ligier and Bonnier, were so far distant and 25 laps down that they failed to be classified.

Not a single car suffered a mechanical failure at the next round of the championship held on a rain soaked Spa circuit in Belgium but unfortunately this phenomenon was not down to some miracle advance in automotive engineering. As torrential conditions swept across the track no less than eight of the 15 starters were involved in two separate crashes on the opening lap. With rain limiting visibility to nothing more than a few feet, first Bonnier, Spence, Siffert and Hulme collided at Burnenville and then Stewart, Hill, Bondurant and Clarke were forced off at the Masta Kink.

Stewart suffered a broken shoulder after being trapped upside down in his BRM but his injuries could have been far worse had Hill not valiantly pulled the petrol drenched driver from his upturned car. Ultimately it was Surtees who overcame the horrendous conditions to take victory from Rindt, Bandini and Brabham.

Surtees' victory at Spa was to be his last for Ferrari. Angered by internal politics he walked out on the team at the Le Mans 24 hour. As the Formula 1 championship moved on to Reims for the French Grand Prix he was back in action – this time behind the wheel of a Cooper-Maserati. His efforts were, however, somewhat short-lived when, after having qualified second, he sped away from the start to take the lead on the first lap and then suffered a fuel pump failure forcing him to abandon. After a hard fought race, Jack Brabham took victory from Surtees' Ferrari replacement Briton Mike Parkes. Brabham's unique Repco engine had come good at last.

The Australian's winning ways continued at the British Grand Prix held at Brands Hatch where he led a Brabham-Repco one-two with team mate Denny Hulme although it should be mentioned that their closest rivals, Ferrari, were unable to attend due to the strikes that were blighting Italian industry. The Maranello racers were, however, back in action as the championship moved on to the Dutch circuit of Zandvoort but once again it was the Brabham pairing who set the pace by taking the first two places on the grid. With the press speculating that Brabham was too old to win the championship for a third time many were amused at the sight of the 40-year-old Australian limping to his car with the aid of a walking stick and a stick-on false beard! For all his joking, Brabham was more than aware that the only true way to silence the doubters was to prove them wrong and this he did by winning the Grand Prix from Graham Hill, who was over a lap behind, and Jim Clark who was distanced by two laps. It was one of the most absolute victories in Grand Prix history.

Brabham continued his winning streak two weeks later at the notorious Nürburgring. Moving to the front on the first lap after qualifying in fifth place his lead was never challenged as the cars swept along the narrow strip of tarmac across the Eifel Mountains.

When the championship moved to Monza a month later it was already clear that the only person in a position to challenge Brabham for the title was Cooper-Maserati's John Surtees. As the drivers battled hard in the opening laps it appeared to be business as usual when the Australian moved to the front on lap four but when mechanical difficulties forced him to retire at the end of the seventh lap the fight for the title was blown wide open. Brabham sat nervously in the pits watching his rival as the race progressed. Surtees had moved up to fourth place behind Scarfiotti, Parkes and Hulme when he entered the pit lane for an unscheduled stop. Climbing out of his cockpit it was clear that Surtees' race was run – his car having developed a fuel leak.

With two races still left to run, Brabham was declared 1966 champion and in doing so became the first and only driver in Grand Prix history to win the title in a car bearing his own name – a record that in this day and age is never likely to be equalled.

ITALIAN GRAND PRIX – MONZA
1967

Before a wheel had turned it was obvious that the 1967 Italian Grand Prix was destined to be one of the classic races of all time. At the sharp end of the action, New Zealand-born Chris Amon was ready to showcase the 48-valve V12 powered Ferrari 312 whilst Honda, having missed the Canadian round some two weeks earlier, was set to field British ace John Surtees in its new RA300 - a thundering machine, affectionately known as the *Hondola*, which utilised the company's brutal new V12 motor on a lightweight Lola chassis that had been built for the Indianapolis 500. Meanwhile Dan Gurney's AAR Eagle-Weslake was equipped with a new, stronger engine which also showed promise. However, it was Jim Clark's unstoppable Cosworth-DFV engined Lotus 49 that proved to be the one to beat come qualification.

Setting out early in the opening session the Scottish farmer from Fife posted a phenomenal 1:28.5 seconds for his 3.57 mile lap of the Monza circuit - a stunning average speed of 145.2mph - whilst 0.3 seconds in arrears was Jack Brabham driving his eponymous BT24-Repco. Third on the grid was Bruce McLaren's BRM powered M5A closely followed by the Ferrari of Amon and Gurney's Eagle. Five different cars were to take the first five places on the starting grid for this Italian epic.

As was typical for any race at the Autodromo Nazionale the start was utter chaos. The flag had not even had the chance to drop before Clark's fellow front-row men sped away with smoke pouring from their tyres. The field soon gave chase but by the end of the first lap it was Australian Brabham who held the lead closely pursued by Gurney and the Lotus of Graham Hill. Clarke, meanwhile, was in fourth having pushed his way back past McLaren's M5A, Jackie Stewart's BRM and Denny Hulme's Brabham-Repco following the opening mêlée. It was then Gurney's turn to briefly take control before Clark finally moved into the lead on the third lap. Gurney tried to stay in contact but was forced to retire on lap five when his Weslake V12 motor expired.

It was now the twin Lotuses of Clark and Hill that led the pair of Brabhams followed closely by Stewart who could see a battle royal unfolding behind him as McLaren, Amon, Surtees and Scarfiotti fought for position on every corner. Next to take the initiative was Hulme who put in a

lap record of 1:28.9 to push his Brabham into the lead just as, further down the field, the great Jochen Rindt took advantage of the confusion to move his Cooper-Maserati into fifth. Hulme's hold of the lead was brief as once more Clark applied the pressure and retook the initiative. Clark wanted this win and wanted it badly. But then disaster struck when, without any warning, the Lotus's handling became erratic and the back started drifting out on each corner. Clark had punctured whilst leading!

Hulme took the lead once more as the Scotsman dived into the pits for an unscheduled wheel change. But, whereas a modern F1 car's wheel can be changed in about half the time it takes you to read this sentence, in 1967 it was a more laboured affair. By the time he was able to rejoin the action Clark was a whole lap down behind his third placed Lotus team mate. Hill and Clark soon took advantage of their more powerful machinery to pass Brabham and it was left to the Englishman to jockey for position with Hulme. The lead changed between the two drivers six times within the next 15 laps but it was too much for Denny Hulme's Brabham and he was forced to retire on lap 30 having overheated.

Once again the Lotus duo took the initiative as Clark moved past Hill and put in lap after blistering lap – breaking the track record with a time equal to that which had earned him his pole position. Dragging along Hill in his slipstream, Brabham was left trailing by a country mile. With 58 of the 68 laps behind them Clark was set to overtake third placed John Surtees in the Honda when disaster struck once more but this time it was Hill's turn for misfortune as his engine expired in spectacular fashion. Unfazed, Clark completed his manoeuvre and all of a sudden found himself in second place behind Jack Brabham. With the bit firmly between his teeth he continued to push hard and, to the amazement of all watching he passed the Australian to take the lead on his 61st circuit having un-lapped himself.

Fate, however, was about to play a cruel hand. With just two corners remaining on the final lap the Lotus started to cough and splutter as the pumps desperately gasped for fuel that wasn't there and Clark could do nothing as he watched Surtees' Honda and Brabham's Repco come storming past in the closing yards to take the top two steps on the podium with just 0.2 seconds separating them. Clark's Lotus rolled in under its own momentum 23 seconds later.

Although Clark's drive may ultimately have been for little reward, there is no doubt that it was, and remains to be, one of the greatest achievements in the history of Grand Prix racing.

ITALIAN GRAND PRIX – MONZA
1969

With many of the Formula 1 regulars consigned to the sidelines due to injury or car development problems, the field at the 1969 Italian Grand Prix was somewhat diminished. The previous year some 24 entrants had taken to the grid in what proved to be one of the hardest fought races ever seen on the Monza track with only six cars making it to the finish line of which just three had covered the full racing distance of 244 miles. This year, however, just 16 cars were set to make the start. With their new flat-12 boxer powered 312B proving difficult to develop, even Ferrari sent just a single machine, a V12 312F1, for their home race.

Qualification under the hot Lombardy sun was as fierce as ever with a succession of quick laps putting the Cosworth DFV powered Gold Leaf Team Lotus of Austrian Jochen Rindt into pole position ahead of Denny Hulme's McLaren and the Matra of Jackie Stewart. With Piers Courage, Bruce McLaren and Jean-Pierre Beltoise filling the remaining top places on the grid, championship contender Graham Hill was left languishing in ninth. Still further back in 12th was the sole Ferrari of Mexican Pedro Rodriguez – the driver having taken over the car after a poor performance during Friday's session at the hands of Ernesto Brambilla. When the drivers lined up for the start just a single second had separated the first five cars on the grid and, as the Italian spectators were about to find out, this closeness of form was about to carry through into the Grand Prix itself.

As the flag dropped it was Jackie Stewart who immediately got the drop on his competitors; powering away from the line and ahead of Rindt and Hulme. Soon there were seven cars in the hunt as the leading three were joined by Courage, McLaren, Beltoise and Siffert in a thrilling high-speed slipstreaming battle of nerves. Rindt managed to move past the Scotsman on lap seven to briefly take control before he too was passed by a fast moving Hulme; his McLaren M7C performing faultlessly. But Stewart was about to play his trump card. With cash primes being offered to the leading driver on certain laps throughout the entire race his Matra technicians had cunningly fitted a fourth gear ratio that offered fantastic mid range punch that would allow him to easily pass his rivals at certain points on the track. With a squeeze of the throttle he was past both

the Lotus and the McLaren and in the money for the first of many times as the race progressed.

The leading seven were now eight – Hill having skilfully carved his way through the field and crossed the gap to the thundering freight train of F1 racers. Courage took his chance and the lead on lap 18 but Stewart easily fought back on the next circuit to once again take the sprinter's bonus. As the frenetic pace started to take its toll on both drivers and cars it was Denny Hulme who was first to fade from the frontrunners as his McLaren started to suffer heavily from brake fade on the high-speed twisting circuit. Next it was Siffert who faltered as his engine gradually lost the power needed to stay in contention, soon followed by Courage whose Brabham coughed and spluttered as its DFV power plant gasped for fuel, the filter having become blocked. Hill's race was over a lap later when his drive shaft broke forcing him to cruise to a standstill soon to be joined by Jo Siffert – his car having finally given up the ghost after 64 laps of the Monza circuit.

And so it was left for the four remaining drivers – Stewart, Rindt, McLaren and Beltoise – to fight it out to the finish. Although it was Stewart who led the foursome in to the start of the final lap it was still clearly anybody's race to win. Rindt wasted no time in being first to pounce as he tore past Stewart and into the lead but the Scot was having none of it. Using all of the track and with his Dunlop tyres struggling for grip on the baking track he managed to re-pass the Austrian within a couple of corners. With no time to rest it was then Beltoise who decided to take the initiative. Braking late into the infamous Parabolica – the final corner on the circuit – he slipped past both the Matra and the Lotus but he was carrying too much speed to maintain his line. Drifting wide on the exit there was nothing more the Frenchman could do as Stewart and Rindt charged past and on towards the line.

For one final time the Scot was able to play the trump card that had allowed him to collect all of the cash bonuses throughout the length of the race. With superior gearing on his side he just managed to punch his way past the Lotus to take victory by 0.08 seconds and the 1969 World Championship. A single second had separated the first five cars on the grid in qualification but just 0.19 seconds separated the first four in the final result.

UNITED STATES GRAND PRIX – WATKINS GLEN
1970

As the Formula 1 teams arrived in Upstate New York for the 1970 United States Grand Prix at the Watkins Glen track, Jochen Rindt's championship lead was almost unassailable. After his unlikely win in an outdated car in Monaco he had gone on to score four straight wins in Holland, France, Great Britain and Germany behind the wheel of the exciting and distinctive Lotus 72. With 18 points on offer in the season's final two Grands Prix only Belgium ace Jacky Ickx on 27 points was in a position to mount an assault on the 45-point tally of the Austrian. The situation was not, however, as clear-cut as it seemed.

Just one month earlier tragedy had struck the world of Formula 1 when, during practice for the Italian Grand Prix at Monza, Rindt's car veered violently to the left under heavy braking at the infamous Parabolica. His Lotus was completely destroyed as it impacted the crash barriers and although the series leader was immediately rushed to hospital he was pronounced dead on arrival. Already that year the championship had been rocked by the deaths of two other star drivers – Jack Brabham having crashed whilst testing a CanAm car at Goodwood and Piers Courage whose De Tomaso-Cosworth had overturned and caught fire in the heat of the action at the Dutch Grand Prix. It had been a dark year for the sport – a fact not lost on title hopeful Ickx.

The opening salvo of the Friday practice session was fired by reigning champion Jackie Stewart driving his spare car – his Tyrrell 001 being confined to the garage whilst undergoing brake and suspension modifications. Soon, however, his times were eclipsed by those of a driver on a mission as Jacky Ickx threw his Ferrari 312 around the 2.35 mile course like a man possessed. With only 15 minutes of dry track time available at the end of a rain-soaked Saturday qualifying practice, Stewart managed to marginally improve on his Friday bet time but it was not enough to unseat the Belgian whose time of 1:03.07 bettered the Scotsman's fastest lap by over half a second. Driving in only his fourth Grand Prix, Brazilian newcomer Emerson Fittipaldi headed up the second row of the grid in his Gold Leaf Lotus having qualified a mere five-thousandths of a second behind Stewart – alongside him was the Yardley Team BRM of Mexican Pedro Rodriguez.

With 100,000 avid spectators lining every straight and bend, the Glen's showman starter, Richard "Tex" Hopkins, strode purposefully across the front of the grid – a huge cigar clenched firmly between his teeth and wearing his trademark lavender suit. As he had done at every major Watkins

Glen race since 1956 he quickly turned and jumped high in the air, green flag in hand, to signify the start of the XIII United States Grand Prix.

As all 24 cars roared away from the start line it was Stewart driving his new Tyrrell 001 who took the early advantage as he out-sprinted Icxk's Ferrari on the opening straight. Rodriguez also took advantage of the Belgian's poor start moving quickly up into second place behind the charging Scot. Close behind the leading trio was Regazzoni, himself hotly pursued by Amon, Surtees and Oliver with Fittipaldi, the victim of an over-cautious start, trailing in eighth place. After just six laps of racing came the first retirement as John Surtees' flywheel broke. Eight laps later it was Oliver's turn to suffer technical difficulties as his engine failed in spectacular fashion. Within another lap Regazzoni had moved past Ickx and into second place but his efforts brought only a brief reward as he was forced to make an unscheduled pit stop to replace a damaged tyre.

With Stewart steadily pulling away from the chasing pack at a rate of a second per lap it was Amon who was next to encounter difficulties when he too experienced tyre problems and was forced to pit for a hasty wheel change. Ten laps later and Ickx too was heading into the pit lane – his Ferrari suffering from a broken fuel line. After a hasty repair and a topping of his tank he was quickly back into the action but, rejoining in 12th place, was clearly out of contention for any hope of championship glory. The running order had remarkably changed again with barely a passing manoeuvre being made by any driver.

But the drama was far from over. On the 76th lap Stewart's Tyrrell started billowing blue smoke from one of its exhaust pipes. The car visibly slowed on the track and soon Rodriguez was catching the Scot at a rate of five seconds each lap. Stewart battled bravely on but he knew it was just a case of waiting for the inevitable to happen and happen it did; on lap 83 his Cosworth engine seized and his race was over.

Rodriguez now led Fittipaldi by almost 19 seconds with just 25 of the 108 laps remaining. All was looking good for the Mexican to take his second win of the season until, on his 100th lap, he coasted into the pit lane with an empty fuel tank. With a splash-and-dash he was soon on his way but it had been enough of a delay to allow the young Brazilian to take the lead and the victory.

With Fittipaldi's rookie team mate Reine Wisell finishing in third place in his debut Formula 1 race it was a good day for Gold Leaf Team Lotus. Not only had they taken the victory and a podium place, they had also secured the Constructor's Championship for the Norfolk team and, most importantly, ensured that Jochen Rindt's name would live on as the 1970 World Drivers' Champion – fortunately the only time in the history of the sport that the title has been awarded posthumously.

ITALIAN GRAND PRIX – MONZA
1971

In this ultra-modern age of hi-tech carbon fibre racing cars packed with more titanium goodies and computing technology than an F16 fighter it is far from uncommon for the result of a race to be decided after just a handful of laps have been completed. What often follows is a drawn out high speed procession resulting in a single car victoriously charging down the finishing straight with not another car in sight. Fortunately Formula 1 has not always been like that; perhaps the greatest example being the culmination of the Italian Grand Prix held on the scorching Monza circuit in the summer of 1971.

Contrary to the expectations of many, the season had not been dominated by the Ferraris of Jacky Ickx, Clay Regazzoni and Mario Andretti. Despite the marque having won the final four races of 1970, Andretti winning the opening round of the 1971 championship in South Africa and Ickx taking victory at a rain-soaked Zandvoort in the Dutch GP, it was Scotsman Jackie Stewart piloting the new Tyrrell 003 who had placed himself as the man to beat. With five wins and a second place in the opening eight rounds placing him an amazing 32 points clear of his nearest rival, his 51-point tally had already secured Stewart his second world title. This early success, however, had not dulled his vigour nor his enthusiasm for the remaining rounds and he arrived at Monza filled with the same level of determination that he had shown throughout the year.

As the teams prepared for race day, Gold Leaf Team Lotus were completely absent from the Monza paddock under threat of manslaughter proceedings from the Italian judiciary following Jochen Rindt's tragic death at the circuit a year earlier. Also missing was Denny Hulme, away on racing duties in the United States, leaving Jackie Oliver as the single driver for Bruce McLaren's racing team. Matra were similarly down to a single car – Chris Amon forced to race alone due to the suspension of Jean Pierre Beltoise following a racing incident in Buenos Aires that had cost the life of Ferrari's Ignazio Giunti. There was, however, excitement at the homecoming of prodigal son Mike Hailwood who, after a successful motorcycle racing career that had seen him lift 10 world titles, had decided to return to four-wheeled motorsport.

As was the norm, unofficial practice on the Thursday was followed by qualifying practice on both the Friday and Saturday. Workmanlike, the drivers steadily improved on their times but it was not until the dying moments of the final session that a rash of super-fast performances suddenly appeared on the timing sheets turning proceedings upside-down. To the dismay of the partisan organisers who had strived to engineer a Ferrari pole position it was, in fact, the lone French Matra of New Zealander Amon that had posted the best time ahead of Ickx – not that you would have known by reading the Italian sporting press who diligently reported that Ferrari had ruled the day! With BRM drivers Jo Siffert and Howden Ganley filling the second row Stewart found himself relegated to seventh whilst Oliver languished in 13th with Hill, Surtees and Hailwood back further still in 14th, 15th and 17th respectively.

After a noisy, dusty and hectic 24-car cavalry charge in the opening lap the order was once again turned on its head as the drivers passed the finish line for the first time. Amon had done a fantastic job at heading backwards through the field – mugged on the first corner he was now back in eighth place – whilst Clay Regazzoni, to the delight of the on-looking Tifosi, had catapulted his Ferrari 312 from eighth on the grid to first on the road. By lap four Peterson was in control having forced his way past the Swiss and into the lead. His position was then usurped by a fast moving Stewart who had pushed hard from the start and was now looking every inch the champion but he was soon to lose his advantage as once again Regazzoni and then Peterson each took control within successive laps.

Lap 15 saw Ickx's Ferrari consigned to the pits with an engine failure – a fate that was to befall Stewart's Tyrrell a single lap later whilst Ickx's team mate, Regazzoni, was forced to retire at the end of lap 17 with similar problems. With both cars out it was not proving to be a good weekend for the Scuderia Ferrari! As Peterson and Cevert traded the lead, lap after lap, Hailwood was making an astonishing charge through the field. Having started near the back of the grid the Englishman moved passed both of the leading cars on lap 25. Peterson was quick to fight back but Hailwood was just as fast in responding as once again the leading positions were shuffled corner by corner. On lap 37 Amon moved past all three to show his intentions of victory but, in a terrible mistake, he unintentionally opened his visor at 180mph and was forced to drop back unable to see.

As the cars lapped the Monza circuit for the 52nd time a new face appeared at the front – that of Briton Peter Gethin in the Yardley Team BRM. Entering the final lap it was Peterson who once again led closely followed by first Hailwood and then Cevert, Gethin and Ganley. In a brave manoeuvre at the Lesmo, Cevert was next to take the lead – an advantage he held until the five cars sped into the infamous Curva Parabolica. With screeching tyres billowing clouds of white smoke Gethin made his move, passing the Tyrrell and running neck and neck with Peterson's March before snatching victory by 0.01 seconds – the smallest winning margin in Formula 1 history – to take his first and only Grand Prix win. So close was the dash for the line that a mere 0.61 seconds separated first place from sixth.

JAPANESE GRAND PRIX – FUJI 1976

The 1976 Japanese Grand Prix on the Fuji circuit marked the culmination of an incident-packed season that had been peppered with excitement, innovation, controversy and tragedy.

The year had started in a confused fashion. Hesketh Racing announced their withdrawal from the sport citing financial difficulties, only to return later in the year thanks to a cash injection from newly found sponsors. Hunt, jobless as the new season approached, was lucky to be snapped up by the well respected McLaren team who had just lost Emerson Fittipaldi – the driver having defected to his brother's team in a decision that stunned the racing world. The surprise of the Brazilian's move, however, paled into insignificance with the sudden and tragic death of racing legend Graham Hill whose life was lost along with those of five of his Embassy team crew when his light aircraft crashed on approach to Elstree Aerodrome.

McLaren had courted their first round of controversy at the hard fought Spanish Grand Prix held at the Jarama circuit on the outskirts of Madrid. Initially the result showed that Hunt had won with a margin of 31 seconds from Ferrari's Austrian superstar and championship leader Niki Lauda. However, scrutineering from FIA officials revealed the Briton's McLaren to be wider than permitted by the Formula 1 regulations of the time. Hunt was disqualified but was later reinstated on appeal although his team received a $3,000 fine for their trouble. A win for Hunt and a rare mechanical failure for Lauda's Ferrari at the French Grand Prix offered the first opportunity for the McLaren driver to close the point gap on the series leader.

McLaren hit the headlines for altogether different reasons as the championship was welcomed back to the British circuit of Brands Hatch. A first corner incident involving two Ferraris left Clay Regazzoni and Ligier's Jacques Laffite sidelined whilst Hunt's McLaren, forced airborne in the impact, suffered badly-damaged suspension. With the race red-flagged Regazzoni and Laffite prepared to restart in their spare cars. Hunt's mechanics, however, elected to quickly rebuild his car whilst officials argued about his eligibility to start. In the ensuing race Hunt finished victorious well over a minute clear of Lauda. Once again he was proclaimed winner but the objections soon

came flooding in as it was claimed he should not have been allowed to take part after his car had received repairs. Initially the protests were rejected by the FIA but, under appeal from Ferrari, they were later upheld and Hunt was stripped of his win.

As the drivers arrived at a typically wet Nürburgring for the German Grand Prix concern was raised once more regarding course safety. This apprehension was proved valid when, on the first lap of the race, Lauda's Ferrari spun and hit a fence before bursting into flames and rebounding onto the track where it was hit first by Harald Ertl's Hesketh and then the Surtees of Brett Lunger.

Hesketh's second driver, Guy Edwards, immediately stopped as did Williams's Arturo Merzario and the four drivers leapt to Lauda's aid – pulling him from the burning wreckage. There is no doubt that their actions save the Ferrari driver's life but, nevertheless, he was seriously burned and was rushed to Adenau hospital for emergency treatment. For a second successive Grand Prix the race was red-flagged and restarted and once again Hunt crossed the finish line in first place but fortunately this time there were no protests to register and the result stood.

With championship leader Niki Lauda hospitalised the series moved to the Osterreichring for the Austrian Grand Prix. Ferrari, still smarting from the events at Brands Hatch a month earlier decided not to race. Also absent from the grid was Formula 1 veteran Chris Amon who, having suffered two accidents already that season and witnessed the shocking incident at the Nürburgring, had decided to hang up his driving gloves for good. A fourth place for Hunt behind unlikely winner John Watson and a win at the following round in Holland signalled the start of his own personal drive for the title.

Monza witnessed the amazing return of Niki Lauda to Formula 1. Bearing horrendous scars he was warmly welcomed back to the paddock by both drivers and fans alike. Proving that the events

of The Ring had not dulled his ability he took a creditable fourth place whilst Hunt span out of contention to keep the Ferrari driver's title hopes alive.

Hunt's charge was revived as the championship moved across the Atlantic with wins in both Canada and at the Watkins Glen track in Upstate New York whilst Lauda, meanwhile, could only manage eighth and third places respectively. In an incredible turn of events the two drivers were set to enter the final round at Japan's Fuji circuit separated by just three points.

Hunt once again caused controversy before the racing had even started when his McLaren team booked a private practice session on the Japanese track which had never before been used for Grand Prix racing but come qualification it was the John Player Team Lotus of America's Mario Andretti that took pole position ahead of the Briton by 0.03 seconds.

When race day arrived so did the weather – so much so that, following the Sunday morning free practice, cancellation looked likely with all the drivers complaining of severe aquaplaning and dangerous conditions. Mindful of incidents earlier in the year the organisers were understandably worried. Even Hunt and Lauda both stated they would prefer not to race. A decision was taken to postpone the start from 1:30pm to 3pm in the hope of an improvement. After an additional delay of five minutes the cars were away although barely able to see from one corner to the next.

Hunt pushed himself into an early lead ahead of Andretti and proceeded to quickly make ground on the Lotus. But then, with the race barely under way Lauda made a move that stunned everyone when he calmly peeled off of the racetrack and into the pit lane. Parking in his garage he climbed out of the car and said "It's just like murder out there, so I'm not going to do it". He still knew that the championship was a possibility but it was now all down to Hunt. Signalled by his pit crew the Englishman began calculating what was required – a third place would guarantee him the title.

Pressing on in the appalling conditions everything looked to be under control until, on lap 20, the rains stopped and the track started to dry. As each lap passed his tyres began to struggle as their wet weather compound began to rapidly overheat. Disaster struck with just 12 laps remaining when his front left completely deflated. Diving into the pits, many, including the Ferrari mechanics, thought his race to be over but the McLaren team rapidly fitted a fresh set of wets and sent him on his way again. Andretti was now in the lead followed by Depailler's Tyrrell, Regazzoni's Ferrari and the Surtees of Alan Jones with Hunt back in fifth. With just a handful of laps remaining it looked as if hopes of the Briton taking the title were fading but then beset by similar tyre problems, first Regazzoni and then Jones were forced to pit for fresh rubber. Hunt crossed the line in third place and as Britain's first World Champion since Graham Hill's triumph in 1968.

SPANISH GRAND PRIX – JARAMA
1981

Ferrari had started their 1981 championship campaign equipped with the all new 126CK. Powered by a high-tech 1.5 litre turbocharged V6 it was both lighter and developed more horsepower than the normally aspirated 3.0 litre flat-12 of the iconic but outdated 312TS it replaced. Its new motor may have been a technological quantum leap for the Maranello factory but when it came to the critical issue of handling, the 126CK was as far from being perfect as could be imagined. By contrast the army of British constructors were experiencing a purple patch in chassis design that more than offset the fact that their Cosworth DFV engines were looking somewhat long in the tooth having been around for the best part of 14 years. It would take a brave and skilled driver to master the Italian thoroughbred and take on the might of the Williams FW07, McLaren MP4 and Brabham BT49C; fortunately for Enzo's team they had Gilles Villeneuve.

The French-Canadian had opened his and Ferrari's account three weeks before the Spanish Grand Prix at Monaco where, in an incident packed race, he had snatched an unlikely victory after race leader Nelson Piquet slid his Brabham into the barriers and the Williams of Australian Alan Jones had suffered fuelling problems. His win may have raised an eyebrow or two in the pit lane and offered welcome relief to the assembled Tifosi but few imagined it was anything more than a stroke of luck for the piano tuner's son from Chambly.

Qualification at the Jarama circuit was a typically frenetic affair as 30 drivers scrapped for the right to place their machinery in one of the 24 places available on the start grid. Front row honours were taken by Jacques Laffite, who put his Ligier in pole position with a time of 1:13.754, and Alan Jones. Close behind was the Australian's Williams team mate, Carlos Reutermann and the McLaren's John Watson. Villeneuve, meanwhile, was back in seventh and on the fourth row behind Alain Prost's Renault, and Bruno Giacomelli, who had done a remarkable job of qualifying his unfancied Alfa Romeo, in a creditable sixth place.

With race-day temperatures touching 37 degrees Celsius, amongst the hottest ever recorded in Formula 1 competition, it was clear from the outset that this was to be as much a battle of

concentration and stamina as it would be a test of driving skill and tactics. As the race started Laffite's superiority in qualification was soon squandered when, suffering from a creeping clutch, he was momentarily left standing on the grid. Capitalising on the situation the twin Williamses of Jones and Reutermann sped into the lead hotly pursued by Villeneuve's charging Ferrari – the Monaco victor having made an astonishing start that had catapulted him into third place before the cars had even reached Nuvolari – the first corner on the circuit. This momentum was carried throughout the lap and it was only a matter of time before the Canadian once again displayed his turbocharged horsepower to move past the Argentinean and into second place as the cars re-entered the pit straight.

With his mirrors filled red with the sight of a chasing Ferrari, Jones decided that it was time to apply some pressure. Driving hard and utilising the dominant handling of his Cosworth-powered Williams he soon started to pull clear and by lap 14 had extended his lead to almost 14 seconds. However, everything was about to change when, in a rare unforced error, the Australian put his car into a spin and shot off the track and into the gravel. Banging his hands on the steering wheel in frustration he was quickly pushed back onto the circuit but the damage was already done and Villeneuve was now leading the race.

With Jones trying hard to work his way back through the field it was now left to Reutermann to save the honour of the Williams garage but, having recovered from his unfortunate start, it was clear that Laffite also had his eyes on the top step of the podium. The Argentinean then began suffering from an intermittent lack of third gear which allowed Laffite to move up into second place whilst Villeneuve continued to defend his lead. Despite the immense power advantage of the Ferrari that permitted the Canadian to show a clean set of heels on the straights he was easily outclassed through the corners. His only hope was to make his 126CK as wide as possible making sure that if anybody was going to pass him they were going to have to go the long way round! Time and time again he was attacked, with Laffite even managing to pull alongside on more than one occasion but, determined to take his second successive victory, he successfully fought off all opposition for an astounding 67 laps to take the win by just 0.21 seconds from the French protagonist. With Watson, Reutermann and de Angelis close behind, just 1.24 seconds separated the first five finishers. Having won behind the wheel of a vastly inferior car Villeneuve had proved that sometimes it's not what you drive but the way you drive it that counts!

UNITED STATES GRAND PRIX WEST – LONG BEACH 1983

When the Formula 1 circus arrived in Long Beach, California, for the 1983 United States Grand Prix West, the drivers were greeted with the unfamiliar sight of a revised track layout. Traditionally the route of this narrow street circuit had taken in a fast section along Ocean Boulevard – one of the city's major thoroughfares – but, in an attempt to improve access and alleviate the traffic problems caused by staging a motor race in a busy urban centre, this had been dropped and replaced by an alternative route taking in Seaside Way and the tunnel underneath the Long Beach Convention Centre. Whilst this new layout looked promising on paper its shortcomings quickly became apparent from the very first moment that an F1 car took to the circuit.

At the point where the new circuit rejoined the old there were two bumps which, to the naked eye, looked insignificant but in reality were severe enough to launch many of the Grand Prix cars at least a foot into the air. Whilst these airborne acrobatics appeared spectacular to the onlooking fans and TV cameras they did for the car's delicate suspension components or the equally delicate constitutions of the drivers. By the end of the first session the teams were expressing their concerns over the state of the track claiming it would be impossible for their cars to complete the race but, despite the controversy and confusion, René Arnoux still managed to post a 1:26.935 second lap to take provisional pole position for Ferrari ahead of the Renault Elf of Alain Prost and his Ferrari team mate Patrick Tambay.

Overnight, the city's Department of Transportation set to work on the problematic area of track so that, thanks to some hard work and a substantial quantity of quick drying cement, by the time the drivers took to the circuit the next day for the final qualifying sessions the offending bumps had been removed. For the majority of the drivers this resulted in a succession of quick lap times but only Tambay was able to better Arnoux's performance from the previous day. Leap-frogging his team mate, the Tifosi were treated to the prospect of an all-Ferrari front row with Keke Rosberg and Jacques Laffite filling row two with their Williamses. As the session progressed one thing became quite apparent; although the Good Year and Pirelli shod cars were performing admirably, those

booted with Michelin rubber were having problems. Alain Prost was the highest placed Michelin runner back in eighth place with Jean-Paul Jarrier and Riccardo Patrese in 10th and 11th respectively. However, this was nothing compared to the woes of the Marlboro McLarens of John

Watson and Niki Lauda. Normally running at the sharp end of proceedings, both drivers found themselves rather unceremoniously dumped on the 11th row in 22nd and 23rd place.

As the lights changed to start the race Tambay got away well and, defending his position into the first corner, set to leading the field. Arnoux, however, was less fortunate as first Rosberg and then Laffite muscled their way past in the opening lap. Braking hard into the first hairpin and with barely a lap covered Rosberg put his Williams into an impressive 360 degree spin before recovering with the loss of just a single place but it was not long before the Finn soon forced himself ahead once more. Meanwhile Michele Alboreto had moved up to fourth in the Benetton Tyrrell relegating Arnoux back to fifth. As the race reached its 22nd lap Jean-Pierre Jarrier pushed Arnoux back yet further and was soon closing in on Alboreto. Unfortunately for the Frenchman he closed a little too quickly and rammed his Ligier into the back of the Tyrrell. Alboreto quickly pitted for repairs as Jarrier continued on.

Four laps later as the leaders approached the hairpin Rosberg decided that he had had enough of following in Tambay's wake and tried to pass but misjudging his line, he clipped his rival's Ferrari sending it airborne and out of the race. Incredibly, with a flick of the steering wheel, the Finn immediately recovered and to all those watching it appeared as if he had got away from the incident scot-free. He had not, however, banked on Jarrier who, having already consigned Alboreto to the pits in his earlier overenthusiastic antics, came barrelling into the side of Rosberg's Williams to take both cars out of the running in an unparalleled display of incompetence.

Laffite was now leading from Patrese with Arrows' Marc Surer lying in third. All eyes, however, had turned on the red and white McLarens of Lauda and Watson who had steadily been carving their way through the field – their tyres proving ever more race-worthy with each passing mile. Both were comfortably past Surer before Watson decided to move ahead on lap 33. With the thundering McLarens bearing down on him, Patrese started to feel the pressure and on lap 44 he overshot a corner and was forced to take to an escape road leaving the door open for an easy pass. The McLarens now just had Laffite to catch. It proved to be a straightforward task for the pair and within a lap Watson was leading with Lauda comfortable in second place. Patrese also managed to pass Laffite but in the latter stages of the race his turbocharger blew and, suffering from a gross lack of power, he gradually drifted back down the field and out of the points.

The McLarens, however, just kept on going and, after 75 laps of racing, passed the finish line to take a stunning 1-2 for the British team having worked their way from the back of the grid. Never had the championship witnessed such an amazing turn of fortune in a single race.

PORTUGUESE GRAND PRIX – ESTORIL
1984

There is an old adage spoken time and time again that reminds competitors that, in the race for a championship title, every point counts. Never more has this rung true than the stunning climax of the 1984 World Drivers' Championship held on the Portuguese circuit of Estoril late in October. It had been another season punctuated by incident and controversy not least that surrounding the rain-soaked Monaco Grand Prix.

Rain had fallen steadily on the Monte Carlo circuit for most of the day resulting in a delay to the start of 45 minutes. No sooner had the field got away than the first incident of the day occurred when the Renaults of Derek Warwick and Patrick Tambay collided on the entry to the first corner – the latter of the two drivers suffering a broken leg in the impact. As the race progressed Alain Prost took control in his McLaren closely pursued by the Lotus of Briton Nigel Mansell whilst Niki Lauda in the other McLaren chased in third. To the delight of his legion of fans Mansell took the lead on lap 11 only to crash heavily into the pit wall just five laps later leaving the McLarens in first and second place. Carving his way through the field was a young driver called Ayrton Senna competing in his first year of Formula 1 – having started in 13th place he was already up to third and closing fast on Lauda. By lap 19 he was ahead of the Austrian whose luck ran out five laps later as he spun on the wet surface and crashed heavily into the barriers at Casino. Closing on Prost at a rate of 1.5 seconds per laps the Brazilian looked unstoppable but even more stunning were the efforts of German newcomer Stefan Bellof who, after starting at the back of the grid, was now himself reeling in both of the frontrunners.

As each lap passed and with the wolves at his door Prost was seen gesturing to the clerk of the course in an attempt to have the race stopped. Then, after just 31 laps and without warning, the red flags appeared and Prost was declared victor. Both Senna and Bellof were incensed feeling rightly that they had both been robbed of a fair chance of victory. With the race having failed to reach half distance, only half of the available points were allocated – Prost taking just 4½ for his trouble instead of the usual 9. This decision would prove critical to one driver's success and another's failure in Portugal.

Lauda arrived at Estoril as championship leader with 5 wins and 66 points to his name. In second was his team mate, Alain Prost, who, despite having taken 7 victories that season, was 3½ points in arrears thanks to the Austrian's ability to constantly score well at each round. To be assured the world title all Lauda had to achieve was a first or second place. For Prost it was a little more complicated – he had to win and Lauda had to finish no higher than third.

Early dampness in qualification gave way to a warm and drying track that saw Nelson Piquet place his Brabham at the front of the grid alongside Prost's McLaren with the Toleman of Senna

and Rosberg's Williams filling row two ahead of the black and gold JPS Lotuses of de Angelis and Mansell. Suffering from turbo problems Lauda could only manage to qualify on the sixth row back in 11th position. His work was cut out!

Piquet's qualifying excellence came to nothing when, as the lights changed, he completely messed up his start and rocketed from pole position to lantern rouge within a handful of seconds. Rosberg was quick to capitalise on the Brazilian's misfortune and soon took control ahead of a charging Mansell, Prost and Senna. As the cars entered their second lap Prost moved up on Mansell and into second place whilst Lauda, starting his long and torturous climb through the field slipped past American Eddie Cheever into 10th. Eight laps later and Prost was in the lead – there was no denying the determination of the man to become France's first world champion!

Ahead of Lauda a battle had developed between Michele Alboreto, Elio de Angelis, Derik Warwick and Stefan Johansson. The Austrian champion-in-waiting, more than aware that often the better part of valour is discretion, decided to sit tight and watch rather than unnecessarily throw himself into the fray. His experience paid dividends when in the following laps both Warwick and Alboreto spun and de Angelis dropped back with tyre problems. Lauda was up to sixth but, meanwhile, Mansell had passed Rosberg for second. For Lauda it was time to attack and a lap later he made a move on Johansson – one so tight that he broke off the front wing of the Swede's Toleman Hart. After seven more laps he was hot on the tail of the battling Rosberg and Senna but these two appeared as nothing more than a minor distraction to the thundering McLaren and both were swept aside with ease.

Prost, however, was still in the driving seat for the title. After 35 laps of racing he led Mansell by a comfortable 10 seconds with Lauda a further 30 seconds back and failing to close. Fifteen laps later Prost looked unstoppable; his lead had increased to 20 seconds with Lauda failing to make inroads into his advantage but his good fortune was about to run out. Mansell, still pushing hard in second, was unaware that his brake fluid was leaking until, on lap 52 he spun. Recovering quickly he was back into the action before Lauda had a chance to pass him but the Austrian had closed the gap down to a few feet. One lap later his brakes failed again and another spin ensued. Lauda was past and into second. There was nothing more Prost could do. He backed off a little to save his car in case Lauda should fail to finish but it was already a fait accompli.

Prost may have crossed the line as winner of the 1984 Portuguese Grand Prix but it was Niki Lauda, finishing in second place, who was World Drivers' Champion. And what was his margin of victory? One-half of a point!

SPANISH GRAND PRIX – JEREZ
1986

The second round of the 1986 season heralded a return to Spanish soil for Formula 1 after an absence of five years. The old narrow Jarama circuit near Madrid had been previously declared unfit for the task of hosting the world's premier motor racing series due to safety concerns. In its place was an all new track carved into the rolling plains just outside the Andalucian city of Jerez de la Frontera.

First to master the 2.76 mile circuit's 13 curves was Brazilian ace Ayrton Senna whose Renault-powered Lotus 98T was better suited to the tight corners and switchback hairpins than the more powerful Williamses and McLarens. Qualifying for the Gran Premio Tío Pepe de España in pole position his time of 1:21.605 was over 0.8 seconds faster than that posted by the Williams of second placed Nelson Piquet. Nigel Mansell headed up row two in the second Williams alongside Alain Prost in his McLaren whilst row three was occupied by Prost's team mate Keke Rosberg and Ligier driver René Arnoux.

As the race started Senna rocketed away along the straight and into the first tight right-hander followed closely by the Williamses of Piquet and Mansell and the McLarens of Rosberg and Prost. Mansell, having lifted off of the throttle due to having concerns over unfavourable in-cockpit fuel consumption readings, soon found himself being passed first by Rosberg and then by Prost. Realising that there was an error with the figures Mansell quickly threw himself back into the action and started hunting down the red and white Marlboro liveried cars ahead. First to fall was Prost who was forced wide by a typically hard Mansell manoeuvre on the brakes into a slow right-hander. Next it was Rosberg's turn for the Mansell treatment as the Brit swept past at the end of the start-finish straight and into third place behind his Williams team mate. But Mansell was waiting for no one and a lap later in a near identical move to that played on Rosberg he was up into second place to the visible frustration of Piquet.

Senna was clearly aware that Mansell was on a charge but there was nothing he could do to prevent the gap from being rapidly closed down. The two cars were soon running together and it was only a matter of time before Mansell was to make his move. As the two drivers caught up with

the Tyrrell of backmarker Martin Brundel, Mansell slipped ahead and soon built up a lead of 4 seconds. Senna fought back and closed the gap and the leading pair was joined by Prost who was now running third after the retirement of Piquet with an overheated engine. The three cars thundered around the track in procession until lap 62 when Senna decided it was time to fight back. Mansell blocked his first attempt but was caught off guard as the three cars approached the hairpin at the back section of the circuit. With the Williams forced well off of its line and Senna already forging ahead, the opportunistic Prost also slipped through the open door pushing Mansell back into third.

It was now that Mansell decided to make a brave tactical decision and with just 10 laps remaining he stormed into the pits for fresh tyres. Rejoining after leaving a smart rubber 11 embedded in the concrete pit lane he was 20 seconds in arrears with 9 laps remaining. At first it seemed like an impossible task but at the end of his first flying lap there was a look of worry on the faces of the Lotus mechanics. Mansell was lapping at a phenomenal four seconds quicker than the two frontrunners.

Prost was soon caught and passed but the lap had cost Mansell an extra 0.7 seconds – it would be right down to the wire! Entering the final lap Senna was just 1.5 seconds ahead with the Briton still closing in fast. He attempted to overtake at the hairpin but it was to no avail as Senna once again made his Lotus appear as wide as a London bus. There was only one thing for it. Could Mansell use his superior power to out-sprint Senna from the final corner? He dived out from the slipstream and made his charge pulling up alongside the Lotus in the final metres. But who had won? Both drivers thought they had taken the victory. Mansell was obviously travelling quicker but that didn't mean that he had been first to cross the line. The tension was unbearable. Then the verdict came: Senna by 0.014 seconds in the second closest Formula 1 result ever.

Mansell's drive had been one of the greatest in the history of the sport but it had been a weird twist of fate that had denied him victory. Prior to the race weekend there had been problems with the official timing gear which had resulted in the finish being moved about 80 metres closer to the final corner. If the finish line had been in its original position then there is no doubt that Mansell would have won. But, as they say, that's racing for you.

AUSTRALIAN GRAND PRIX – ADELAIDE
1986

For the second year running the culmination of the Grand Prix season was scheduled to take place in Australia. Despite a long and illustrious history of producing some of the world's best drivers it was only after 35 years of competition that the nation had finally been granted its own race. Air travel was faster and more economic and TV coverage guaranteed global exposure. Like Monaco and Long Beach, the Adelaide track, based around the city's Victoria Park, was a tight and twisting street circuit of the old-school full of thunderingly fast straights, 90 degree turns and stop-go switchbacks.

With just this one round left to run, Nigel Mansell was leading the Drivers' Championship on 70 points with a tally of 5 wins but he had far from dominated the season. Hot on the Briton's heels with 63 points to his name was his Williams-Honda team mate Brazilian Nelson Piquet whilst just a single point further in arrears was reigning champion Alain Prost of the McLaren team. The prospect of three drivers being in with a chance of the title had the journalists and pundits reaching for their calculators and working out the possible permutations.

With a seven-point advantage and only nine points on offer for a win there was no doubt that Mansell was the hot favourite. This was reinforced in qualification when the man from Surrey put his Williams FW11 on pole position with a time of 1:18.403. However, joining him on the front row was Piquet whilst Prost was just a row behind – separated on the timing sheets from the frontrunners by a remarkable performance by Ayrton Senna in an underpowered Lotus 98T.

Charging away from the grid surrounded by a shower of sparks from the titanium skid plates fitted to the cars of the era and with the Drivers' title firmly in his sights Mansell could not have done worse. Heading into the second corner he was forced to yield to Senna who, although well out of the running for championship glory, was determined as ever to place himself on the top step of the podium. Mansell then found himself being passed first by the Williams of his team mate and next by Keke Rosberg's Tag-McLaren. Now in second place Piquet decided that he was not in the mood for hanging about and immediately attacked Senna's lead. Making good use of his

superior power he was quickly through, becoming third race leader with less than one 2.35 mile lap covered.

As the cars stormed along the Adelaide street circuits pit straight for the second time Rosberg moved swiftly ahead of Senna. Mansell, meanwhile, was still running in fourth place but after another two laps he too sped past the underpowered Lotus to move up to third – a position which could not only secure him a place on the podium but also the title. Another two laps passed before Prost, also contending title honours, moved ahead of Senna. The shuffling, however, was far from over. Just one more lap into the race and Rosberg attacked for the lead. As his tyres struggled for grip he slid his McLaren inside the Williams to take control of the race.

Winner at Adelaide the year before and also having victories at Monaco and Detroit in his palmares, Rosberg was a past master on tight street circuits. Putting his expertise to good use he was soon pulling away from the rest of the field. On lap 23 Piquet instantly demoted himself from a steady second to fourth place behind Mansell and Prost with a spectacular spin. Prost's advantage over the Brazilian was, however, short lived when four laps later he punctured and was forced to pull in for fresh rubber. Quick work by his mechanics meant that he was able to rejoin in fourth place but for all those watching his hopes of a championship title did not look good.

Following his spinning antics Piquet had the bit grasped firmly between his teeth. With each lap that passed he gradually ate into Mansell's advantage until, on lap 44, they were together. Knowing that a third place would secure the championship Mansell reluctantly let him through and in to second. Prost was also pulling back lost ground and on lap 57 made contact with the other two title contenders. They were now running like a train in second, third and fourth but the advantage was still with the Englishman.

Rosberg's substantial lead looked secure until lap 63 when his tyre de-laminated throwing chunks of rubber into the air. Unable to continue there was nothing he could do but park his beleaguered McLaren at the trackside and spectate. Promoted to second place, the situation now looked even better for Mansell. With Ayrton Senna having retired with engine problems there was a considerable gap back to Stefan Johansson's Ferrari in fourth. All he needed to do was finish in the top three and Prost and Piquet's positions would be irrelevant.

Then it happened; one of the most iconic moments in motor racing history. With his Williams travelling at over 180mph Mansell's left rear tyre exploded sending debris and sparks everywhere. Fighting hard for control he unbelievably managed to steer the crippled machine towards an escape road and to safety. In an instant, his championship hopes were over.

Fearing that the problems that had caused him to crash might also affect the second Williams, Piquet was quickly brought into the pits for new tyres. Rejoining in second place the Brazilian tried bravely to regain lost ground but it was to be in vain when, after 82 laps of hard racing, Alain Prost crossed the finish line as winner of the Australian Grand Prix and 1986 World Drivers' Champion.

MEXICO GRAND PRIX – HERMANOS RODRIGUEZ 1990

Heavy rains had battered the Hermanos Rodriguez circuit for most of the afternoon and night preceding the first free practice session on Friday morning. And so, despite the clear blue skies and brilliant sunshine, the assembled drivers were greeted with a damp track that would prove to be perilously slippery for some. First to fall victim was Aguri Suzuki who could do little to prevent his Lola-Lamborghini spinning helplessly into the crash barriers at 135mph. Remarkably the Japanese driver was able to leap unscathed from the wreckage and jog his way back to the pits to head straight on out in the team's spare car.

Qualification saw Gerhard Berger set the fastest time of the weekend after managing to find a clear, traffic-free lap for his McLaren early during Friday's first session. His time of 1:17.227 was almost a quarter of a second faster than that of Riccardo Patrese's Williams; the Italian having improved from third to second on Saturday afternoon leapfrogging Berger's team mate Ayrton Senna in the process. Joining Senna on the second row of the grid was Nigel Mansell – the Briton having moved to Scuderia Ferrari the previous season. His own team mate, reigning triple world champion Alain Prost, was languishing back in 13th place – his lowest grid position since his 1980 debut season – having suffered setup problems all weekend. Trying to maintain a brave face he claimed that a good race tyre was more important than a good grid position.

For all of Prost's bravado few spectators considered him to be a threat starting, as he was, from such a lowly position. As far as they were concerned the smart money lay with Senna who, although tucked away on the second row, had already won three of the five Grands Prix contested that season.

Berger's qualification advantage was quickly removed at the start when Riccardo Patrese made the perfect getaway from the line followed quickly into the first corner by a charging Senna – the cautious Austrian perhaps distracted by the fact that at the previous round in Montreal he had made a jump-start and subsequently been issued with a one-minute penalty.

GREATEST MOMENTS OF GRAND PRIX

As the cars battled on throughout the first lap the tenacious Senna tried time and again to slip his McLaren past the Williams of Patrese but as they headed towards completing their first lap it was still the Italian who maintained control. Then Senna pounced – diving out of the slipstream he at last pulled alongside as the pair sped across the finish line for the first time. Into corner one again and this time it was Senna who led having unleashed the superior power of his Honda motor. Unsettled, Patrese was then caught out by Berger in the second McLaren as the Austrian immediately slipped through into second place. Things quickly went from bad to worse for the Williams driver as next Piquet and then Thierry Boutsen muscled their way ahead. Meanwhile Prost was carving his way through the field and was challenging Derek Warwick for eighth.

Berger's time near the sharp end of the race was temporarily cut short when, on lap 12, his front left tyre started to blister and he was forced to head into the pits for fresh rubber. Fast work by the McLaren mechanics helped him swiftly rejoin but he was now relegated to 12th.

As Prost had predicted the Goodyear tyres were beginning to perform well as both Ferraris started to make light work of the opposition. Quick to fall to their two-pronged attack was the Williams of Patrese – passed first by Mansell on lap 22 and then by Prost four laps later by which time the Englishman was already ahead of Boutsen in the second Williams car. Prost followed suit on lap 31 and the pair began to reel in Nelson Piquet's second-placed Benetton – Mansell being first to go ahead on lap 36, his team mate making the double six laps later after the Benetton was forced to pit for new tyres.

Prost was now moving faster than ever and swept past Mansell as the pair approached a slow moving backmarker. Senna, meanwhile, was still out ahead but he was starting to experience problems as a slow puncture wreaked havoc with his handling. Then, with an almighty explosion, his tyre gave out forcing another early retirement for the unlucky Brazilian gifting the lead to Prost who had made a remarkable recovery from his 13th-place start.

Berger, meanwhile, had been making his own charge back through the field and, with just three laps remaining caught and passed a surprised Mansell. The Briton immediately fought back in a relentless attack forcing the Austrian to defend at every moment. Then, with just over a lap remaining, he executed one of the most memorable and daring passes in Grand Prix history when he swept past on the outside of his opponent on the infamous Peralta at 150mph forcing Berger to lift off to avoid a major collision. Berger continued to hound Mansell all the way to the line but there was nothing he could do to retake the position he had lost and he had to settle for third place behind the superlative Ferraris.

EUROPEAN GRAND PRIX – DONINGTON PARK
1993

When the Formula 1 circus arrived at Donington Park for the third round of the 1993 World Championship it was the first time that the premier motor racing class had graced the Derbyshire circuit since 1938. On that occasion it was the great Tazio Nuvolari of Italy who had reigned supreme behind the wheel of an all conquering Auto-Union Type D – the original Silver Arrows. The 1993 race proved to be no less exciting as once again a single driver dominated proceedings in what is generally held to be one of the greatest Grand Prix performances in the history of the sport.

Alain Prost had won the opening round of the championship under clear skies at South Africa's high altitude Kylami track. He had demonstrated that, in no uncertain terms, the Williams-Renault was the car to beat. But the applecart had been upset just a fortnight later when, in a chaotic race held in atrocious conditions, Ayrton Senna had taken victory, the 100th for McLaren, whilst Prost had squandered his pole position advantage having crashed on lap 29.

Prost was back on the front of the grid at Donington. Alongside him was his team mate Damon Hill who was competing in his second Formula 1 season having just joined to replace Nigel Mansell who had decided to try his hand in the US Indy Car series. Heading up the second row was another relative newcomer to the sport – Michael Schumacher – who was enjoying his second full season with Benetton-Ford. To his side was championship leader Ayrton Senna.

Weather conditions for race day morning were appalling. It was obvious that all of the cars would need to start on wet tyres but for how long? Wet weather tyres are designed purely for use in the rain relying, as they do, on the standing water to cool the special soft compound grooved rubber. Using them on a dry track would cause rapid deterioration risking handling problems, blowouts or worse.

As the lights changed from red to green and the field accelerated towards Redgate, Prost and Hill made their predictably good start. Senna, meanwhile, found himself boxed in behind the

GREATEST MOMENTS OF GRAND PRIX

Austrian Karl Wendlinger who had passed the Brazilian almost immediately the field had got underway. Wendlinger's charge continued and before the first corner he was also ahead of Schumacher. Senna, however, was about to launch a stunning attack.

By the time the cars were exiting Redgate he was already in front of Schumacher. Then, heading down through the perilous Craner Curves he was up alongside Wendlinger before moving ahead on the entry to the Old Hairpin. Charging up the hill under Starkey's Bridge he rapidly closed in on an unsuspecting Damon Hill before making his move up the inside of the British driver at McLeans. Prost was now in his sights as the cars stormed along Starkey's Straight and through the Esses. Approaching the Melbourne Hairpin he moved alongside and then, as the cars turned in, he forced his way through once more and into the lead. Senna immediately started to stretch out a lead. At the end of the second lap he already had a 4.25 second advantage over Prost and within another lap this was extended to almost 7 seconds.

GREATEST MOMENTS OF GRAND PRIX

Conditions changed on lap 7 when the sun started to shine and a dry line became visible. First to pit for slick tyres was Ligier's Martin Brundle but his tactics proved rather premature when he spun his car in the damp on his out lap and was forced to retire. Hill, running in third place pitted on lap 10 followed by Senna and then Prost. Senna was quickly back out on track, this time on slick tyres, and continued to defend a lead of about five seconds.

By lap 20 he was already catching backmarkers when the rain once more started to fall heavily on the track. Hoping to gain some advantage Prost was quick to pit for a fresh set of wets whilst on track both Schumacher and Mark Blundell spun off. Hill chose to pit on lap 23 but Senna just kept on going on slick rubber – incredibly posting faster lap times than his wet-shod opponents. Satisfied that he had gained enough advantage he eventually came in for new tyres still managing to rejoin the fray in first place after the stop with 15 seconds in hand.

Once more the track started to dry and on lap 31 Prost was in for another pit stop and fresh slicks. This time Senna chose to pit at the same time but an uncharacteristic slow change by his McLaren mechanics saw him rejoin the action behind Prost. But this would only last for four laps as again the heavens opened and the Frenchman charged into the pits for wets on lap 35.

With slicks still fitted to his car Senna stayed out regardless setting faster and faster lap times against all odds. Ten laps on and the track started to dry yet again. Prost attempted his sixth change of tyres but disaster struck when, hurrying to get back into the action, he stalled his McLaren. Wasting valuable seconds as the mechanics attempted to re-start his car, he could do nothing but watch as his Brazilian rival sped past his stranded car to lap him.

Having at last decided to change to new slicks Senna headed into the pits but as he did so spots of rain started to fall. Waving at his mechanics he continued to drive straight through and back onto the track having lost little time in the process. Hill was now closing at three seconds per lap allowing the Briton to un-lap himself with just 10 laps remaining. On lap 66 Senna went in for his final set of wets. Rejoining well ahead there was nothing the field could do to stop him speeding on to victory with only Damon Hill finishing on the same lap. Rubens Barrichello had managed to move up to third place following Prost's dreadful pit stop but the unfortunate Brazilian's hopes of his first podium finish were dashed when his fuelling system malfunctioned with just two laps remaining.

Senna's astounding victory had seen him out-drive his opponents in the most amazing demonstration of wet weather driving since Jackie Stewart's astounding Nürburgring drive back in 1968.

EUROPEAN GRAND PRIX – NÜRBURGRING
1995

By 1995 the days of the full 14 mile Nordschleife with its 100 treacherous bends twisting their way through Germany's Eifel Mountains were long in the past. The ultimate drivers' circuit had last been used for a Formula 1 race back in 1976 after which the German Grand Prix had switched location to the infinitely safer but somewhat sterile Hockenheimring. A shorter 2.8 mile Nürburgring circuit, the *GP-Strecke,* was, however, completed in 1984 and had since become a regular home for the Grand Prix of Europe. Although it paled in comparison to its legendary predecessor it was a state of the art modern circuit built wholly with the safety of both drivers and spectators in mind.

The 1995 championship had been brought to life by a fantastic battle for supremacy between Benetton's controversial German ace Michael Schumacher and Williams's home-bred hero Damon Hill. Schumacher had undoubtedly dominated proceedings having already taken six victories to Hill's three within the first 13 rounds of the competition but the war of attrition that raged between the two drivers had kept fans on the edge of their seats and sparked countless debates over the merits of each driver's sometimes unconventional methods and tactics.

Qualification for the European Grand Prix had seen Hill pipped to the post by his Williams team mate, David Coulthard, who was riding on a wave of self-confidence having taken top honours over Schumacher in Estoril just a week before. Schumacher was, therefore, relegated to the second row of the grid alongside Ferrari's Gerhard Berger whilst Jordan's Eddie Irvine and Jean Alesi in the second of the Prancing Horses filled the third.

Heavy rain had battered the GP-Strecke on the morning of the race and, although the showers had ceased long before the start, most of the teams elected to take to the grid on full wets. Only Ferrari and McLaren were exceptions to the rule opting for slick tyres and dry weather suspension and wing settings in the hope of the quick formation of a dry racing line.

David Coulthard's getaway from the grid was exceptional as was Schumacher's – the German slipping comfortably into second place by the time the field reached the first corner as Hill, starting

off of the racing line, struggled for grip on the wet and greasy tarmac. As expected, both Ferraris dropped back through the field as did the McLarens – the difference being that although Alesi and Berger were relegated to sixth and ninth respectively McLaren's Mika Hakkinen and Mark Blundell found themselves being passed by all and sundry before taking up positions as honorary back markers.

Ferrari's tactics started to pay off as the race approached its 12th lap – a dry line was forming and Maranello's best were starting to make progress through the field. First to fall was Schumacher's Benetton team mate Jonny Herbert, next was the Jordan of Eddie Irvine. The charging Alesi was

already up to fourth place before being catapulted into a 20 second lead as Coulthard, Schumacher and Hill headed into the pits for slick rubber and a splash of fuel.

Once out of the pits Hill immediately started to attack Schumacher – his car obviously faster with fresh tyres and a full fuel load. Unsurprisingly Schumacher was not in the mood to capitulate. Making his car as wide as possible and holding defensive lines into every corner it seemed impossible for the popular Briton to make a move past the German master. Trying a little too hard Damon was forced to lock his wheels to avoid a collision on more than one occasion but he would not give up. Giving Schumacher a taste of his own ruthless medicine he forced his way ahead and into third place but soon lost his hard-fought advantage – almost spinning at the final corner to allow his rival the opportunity to effortlessly slip past. This time Schumacher seized his chance to pull away.

Ahead Coulthard was starting to experience problems of his own as the heavy fuel load upset the handling of his car – the Scot having been forced to start in his spare car following an incident in the pre-race warm-up lap. Schumacher wasted no time in bearing down on the second Williams and was quick to pass the ailing FW17 – his move duplicated by the chasing Hill just a single lap later.

Alesi, meanwhile, continued to press on ahead with his lead now extended to a healthy 30 seconds and half distance approaching. Diving into the pits for his scheduled tyre and fuel stop he rejoined with Hill close on his tail – Schumacher having elected to make his stop at the same time. Recognising that he had an opportunity to distance the German, Hill chose to attack Alesi but, in an ill-timed attempt at passing he damaged his nose cone and was forced to pit on the next lap.

Schumacher, meanwhile, had decided that a safe second place was not good enough and started to post lap after blistering lap at breakneck speed to gradually reel in Alesi's wayward Ferrari. Each time he passed the finish line the margin was slashed yet again. Hill too was keen to make up for lost time but he paid for his over-exuberance with a heavy crash into the barriers and was forced to retire.

With just three laps remaining Alesi's mirrors were filled with the sight of Schumacher's blue and yellow Benetton until, approaching the tight left-right chicane, the German made his move. Running audaciously fast into the corner he forced his way inside Alesi's car. With their wheels overlapping and perilously close to making contact there was nothing the Frenchman could do but surrender his position. Schumacher was through and on his way to his seventh victory of the season and his second World Drivers' Championship.

DAMON HILL'S WORLD CHAMPIONSHIP
1996

The 1996 Championship was a breath of fresh air for Damon Hill's legion of fans who had spent the previous two seasons watching their hero play second fiddle to the Teutonic genius of Benetton's Michael Schumacher. In 1994 Hill arrived at Adelaide for the final race of the season just a single point in arrears of championship leader Schumacher but having won four out of his five previous races. Obviously recognised as the driver in form, the smart money was on Hill taking the title but it was not to be. On lap 35 his car controversially collided with Schumacher's relegating both to the sidelines. In an instant Hill's title hopes had ended and Schumacher was World Drivers' Champion. To many, the German's actions were seen as foul play whilst to others it was simply an unfortunate racing incident. Whatever the truth, it was a bitter disappointment.

A year later and Hill had once again finished second in the championship to Schumacher although this time the margin was far greater. The Williams driver had finished on the top step of the podium on no less than four occasions but this was nothing compared to the nine winner's trophies that had been collected by his rival. Hill's championship had been blighted by a series of high profile errors which included collisions with Schumacher at both Silverstone and Monza. For his employer, Frank Williams, his card was already marked and it became clear that 1996 would be his final year with the Oxfordshire-based team. Realising that the future of his career was in jeopardy he set to making 1996 a year to remember for Williams, his fans and the British public.

Making his Formula 1 debut at Melbourne's Albert Park circuit, Williams's new boy, Jacques Villeneuve, had stunned everyone by taking pole position ahead of his veteran team mate. As the race progressed Villeneuve set a thundering pace ahead of Hill but mechanical problems forced the Canadian to lift off allowing the Briton through to take victory and 10 points.

Damon Hill's triumph in Australia may have been partly down to Villeneuve's misfortune but his performance at the Brazilian Interlagos track three weeks later were nothing short of genius. Qualifying almost a second faster than his nearest rival he went on to take his second successive victory 18 seconds ahead of second-placed Jean Alesi in monsoon conditions that left rivers running across the track, and had the pleasure of lapping Schumacher in the process.

A week later and Hill's form and good fortune continued with another pole position and race victory having led proceedings from start to finish. Once more he had demoralised Schumacher who had closely stalked the Williams driver until lap 15 when Hill decided it was adios amigo and put his foot down building up a six second lead in just four laps. Even after the field had been forced to bunch up behind the safety car and his advantage lost it was simply a case of getting back to business and pulling clear once the track was deemed safe for racing. Hill's dominance had been complete and it was three out of three for Britain's new hope.

Although confident of achieving his fifth straight win (having also won the last race of the 1995 season) Hill's luck ran out at the European Grand Prix held on Germany's Nürburgring. After an appalling start from pole that Hill admitted was no fault other than his own, he failed to recover

his position and was relegated to finishing fourth although the Williams team was still jubilant, victory having been taken by Villeneuve in only his fourth Formula 1 start.

Hill made amends at Imola. Starting second on the grid alongside his arch rival, Schumacher, the pair were trumped at the start by McLaren's David Coulthard who sped away to take an early lead. For 20 laps the Scot fought hard with the German as Hill sat comfortably behind before pouncing and taking control. When Schumacher pulled into the pits Hill put his foot to the floor gaining enough time to make his own stop and still rejoin at the head of the race. It was a satisfying victory and one which extended his championship lead to 21 points after just five races.

Despite claiming pole positions at both Monaco and Spain, Hill was unable to score points in his next two races. A rare mechanical failure denied him victory on the Monte Carlo streets and an unfortunate spin in the wet on the Catalunya circuit had forced an unwelcome early retirement handing victory to Michael Schumacher. Whereas a bout of bad luck like this would have rattled Hill in previous seasons, here he was a new man; more confident and more committed than ever before.

GREATEST MOMENTS OF GRAND PRIX

The Canadian Grand Prix saw Hill back in charge once more with yet another pole position and race win ahead of his Williams team mate. This was followed by yet another victory as the championship moved to France and the Magny Cours circuit. Villeneuve may have been denied a home win in Montreal but the young Canadian was quick to respond taking his second career win at Silverstone after Hill was forced to retire when technical problems with his car caused him to spin out early in the race.

Hill's 20th career victory and seventh win of the year came at Hockenheim in front of Michael Schumacher's rather partisan home crowd. It was not an easy race for the Briton having been trapped behind Berger and Alesi after a bad start. An efficient pit strategy had helped him past the Frenchman and into second place but it was a bit of luck combined with a blown engine on Berger's Benetton that handed him the victory.

A second place behind Villeneuve in Hungary and a fifth behind Schumacher at Spa marked the start of a worrying dry patch for Hill. Although leading the championship his team mate was closing at a rate of knots with his advantage reduced to just 13 points with three races left to run. This was compounded at the Italian Grand Prix when Hill clipped a tyre wall, spun his car and stalled. It was a silly mistake that could have cost him dear but to his relief Villeneuve only managed to finish out of the points in seventh place whilst victory went to Schumacher who was no threat to the title race.

Villeneuve did, however, close the gap further in the penultimate round at Estoril. Hill took pole position for the 10th time that year but the Canadian, sensing that the title could be within his grasp, drove an astounding race to better his team mate by almost 20 seconds at the finish having stolen the lead during the half distance pit stops.

Going into the final round at Japan's Suzuka circuit, both Williams drivers had everything to play for. Hill was ahead in the championship by nine points but Villeneuve could still take the title if he won the race and Hill failed to score any points. It was a nervous time for them both. Villeneuve made his intentions clear by taking pole position by 0.4 seconds from Hill but a poor race start saw him immediately relegated to fifth place. Hill meanwhile was stepping out at the front of the field determined to win the race and the title. Then, after 37 laps of racing, Jacques Villeneuve's right rear wheel sheered off at the hub and his race and title hopes were over.

As the number 5 Williams passed the pit lane at the start of lap 38 its driver glanced across to read his pit board – it simply said "Damon Hill 1996 World Champion".

JAPANESE GRAND PRIX – SUZUKA
1997

Having taken the top spot on the podium in Brazil, Argentina, Spain, Great Britain, Hungary, Austria and Luxembourg, Jacques Villeneuve found himself in the enviable position of leading the World Drivers' Championship as the 1997 season headed into its penultimate round at the Japanese circuit of Suzuka. But the Canadian was far from home and dry in the race for the title. Lurking perilously close was the indomitable and on-form Michael Schumacher who, although having won just four Grands Prix to Villeneuve's seven, was just eight points in arrears having completed more races in the points. With just two rounds remaining some sort of showdown was inevitable.

The timing sheets at the end of qualification showed few surprises. Jacques Villeneuve had, for the ninth time that season, taken pole position in his Williams-Renault shadowed, as always, by the Ferrari of his arch rival Schumacher in second place. Heading up row two was the German's Ferrari team mate, Eddie Irvine. Alongside the Irishman was the first of the McLaren-Mercedes driven by Mika Hakkinen whilst the third row featured Gerhard Berger's Benetton and Heinz-Harald Frentzen in the second Williams. At first glance it looked like business as usual but an incident in qualifying was about to throw a whole new complexion over the weekend that would see tactics take precedence over pure racing.

During the Saturday morning session Jos Verstappen's Tyrrell-Ford had come to an untimely stop on the apex of the Spoon Curve just before the back straight. The rules of racing specifically state that under a waved yellow flag drivers must slow down, not overtake and be prepared to change direction or follow an unusual line. To the chagrin of the FIA, Villeneuve had developed an unwelcome habit of ignoring waved yellows and, as might have been expected, charged straight through without lifting off the power – a highly dangerous move. For the competition organisers it was an infraction too many. He had been cited for similar offences on three other occasions that season alone and was already under the shadow of a suspended one-race ban. The officials had no choice but to exclude him from the next day's racing.

Williams-Renault had a dilemma on their hands. An appeal could be costly and embarrassing but if Villeneuve failed to compete their championship hopes could be in tatters. Figuring that it was better to race and lose the appeal than not race at all, the team made their protest and Villeneuve was allowed to start. But it left open a whole new tactical quandary – not only for the Oxfordshire team but also for their wealthy Maranello counterparts.

From the start Villeneuve's plan became apparent. As the lights changed and the cars sped away from the grid the Canadian slew his car into the path of Schumacher's Ferrari blocking off any

opportunity for the German to take an early lead. But, rather than setting the blistering pace that in previous races had seen the whole field strung out within the first few laps, Villeneuve seemed to be touring. Fast touring, yes, but nothing akin to the race pace that would be expected from the championship leader. His plan was simple; he wanted other drivers to attack Schumacher and take on the race so that, regardless of the outcome of his appeal, the German's quest for points would be impinged.

But nobody was taking the bait. Rather than launching the opportunistic attacks that Villeneuve had predicted the entire field formed an orderly queue behind the Williams and the Ferrari. Frustrated, Villeneuve found himself at the centre of an impasse. What he had not banked on was that the Ferrari team had a plan of its own which its drivers were about to spring.

On the second lap Irvine, who had been relegated to fourth place in the opening lap mêlée, sped past both Hakkinen and Schumacher – the latter being more than complicit in aiding the manoeuvre. Filling the mirrors of Villeneuve's Williams he then attacked again. The Canadian tried to block him on the entry to the chicane but the Northern Irishman was ready and drove hard around the outside and into the lead. Demonstrating just how lacklustre a pace Villeneuve had been setting, Irvine was already 5.3 seconds ahead after a single lap and 12 seconds clear two laps later. Villeneuve still continued to lap slowly, hoping in vain that at least one other driver would attack Schumacher and set off in pursuit of the wayward Irvine. Finally, on lap seven, he realised this was just not going to happen and started to chase.

Villeneuve's plans continued to fall apart in the first round of scheduled pit stops when, thanks to a superb effort by the Ferrari mechanics, Schumacher's F3108 re-emerged onto the track ahead of the Canadian's Williams. It was now time for Ferrari to execute the second part of their plan. Irvine, 11 seconds in the lead, slowed his car to allow his team mate to catch up and pass. As soon as he was through he set to blocking Villeneuve's path allowing Schumacher to pull out a considerable lead.

Villeneuve made one more attempt at getting past Irvine during his final pit stop but a problem with the fuel nozzle lost him precious seconds ultimately relegating the Canadian to fifth place whilst Schumacher went on to take victory ahead of Frentzen's Williams thanks to an amazing display of team tactics and precision timing.

BELGIAN GRAND PRIX – SPA FRANCO CHAMPS
2000

Despite having won more rounds of the 2000 World Drivers' Championship than any other competitor, Ferrari's Michael Schumacher was not leading the race for the title as the series arrived at the Belgian circuit of Spa Franco champs. That honour was held by McLaren's Mika Hakkinen who, with three wins and five second-place finishes to his name, led the German by two points. Waiting in the wings just a further four points in arrears was Hakkinen's square-jawed Scottish team mate David Coulthard who had also achieved three wins within the opening 13 rounds.

With qualification held under beautifully clear skies, Mika Hakkinen took his fifth pole position of the year with an advantage of almost 0.8 seconds over second-placed Jarno Trulli with Jenson Button, racing in his first season of Formula 1, and Michael Schumacher filling the second row. However, the Finn had benefited from a clear, traffic-free lap whilst the majority of the field, including the other championship frontrunners, had had to contend with waved yellow flags at the bus-stop chicane which undoubtedly had taken the edge off their performances. Hakkinen conceded that his advantage was not as great as it seemed and that the race would be hard fought from start to finish.

In the early hours of Sunday morning, the day of the race, it started to rain very hard and by dawn the heavy showers had been joined by a rising mist that sat low over the undulating circuit. It was still raining as the drivers set out for their free practice session. Lapping in the atrocious conditions at over 13 seconds slower than the previous day it was a grim reminder to the drivers of just how difficult a circuit Spa is to master. When it bites it bites hard as was found out by Giancarlo Fisichella who was lucky to emerge unscathed from the wreckage of his Benetton after crashing heavily into the Armco at the Stavelot curve.

By the time the race was due to start the rains had ceased but the track was still perilously wet and the decision was taken to invoke a rolling start. As the safety car switched off its flashing lights and headed into the pits Hakkinen was away and making good use of the clear track ahead and the confusion thrown up from the dense spray enveloping the field behind. Meanwhile, Michael

Schumacher moved ahead of Button at the chicane after the Briton got out of line in a brave attempt to pass Trulli's Jordan. By the next corner Schumacher was ahead of Trulli. Once more Button attempted the pass but this time he made contact sending the luckless Italian into a spin and out of the race. Button recovered to resume in fifth having gifted third to his team mate Ralf Schumacher.

After five laps a dry line was starting to form and the sun was shining brightly. Hakkinen had extended his lead to 10 seconds as the first of the cars, Jean Alesi's Prost-Peugeot, headed into the pits to change to slicks. A lap later and Schumacher was also running on fresh rubber and on lap seven Hakkinen made the inevitable stop.

It was soon clear to those watching that Schumacher's dry setup was far better than that of Hakkinen's McLaren and he began to close the gap on the flying Finn. Hakkinen responded well but on lap 13 made an unforced error by touching a wet curb at Stavelot and putting his car into a spin. Remarkably, he managed to control his high-speed skid but, having briefly ended up on the grass, his five second advantage over Schumacher was instantly converted to a five seconds deficit.

On lap 22 and now 11 seconds ahead of Hakkinen, Schumacher made the second of his scheduled pit stops. Five laps later the McLaren also headed in. With new tyres and a quick tweak of the front wing, Hakkinen sped back out onto the track but now, thanks to the efforts of his mechanics, he was just seven seconds behind and starting to close in. Lap after lap the gap was reduced until, with just four circuits remaining, Hakkinen was running deep in Schumacher's slipstream.

Powering out of L'Eau Rouge Hakkinen made his move. Closing fast down the back straight he started to sweep inside Schumacher but the German was not willing to give in that easily and swept across to close the door on his opponent – the cars just inches apart at over 300kmh. Hakkinen immediately regrouped himself and prepared to try again.

Once again it was L'Eau Rouge that provided the springboard but this time as Schumacher and Hakkinen charged along the back straight there was something new to contend with – they were about to lap the BAR of Ricardo Zonta. Schumacher waited until the last possible moment before swinging out to overtake in another attempt to close the door on his rival but Hakkinen had a plan of his own and dived up the inside of Zonta and into the lead.

Three laps later Schumacher had to settle for a valiant second place whilst victory went to a deserving Hakkinen after one of the bravest and most spectacular overtakes in motor racing history which even Schumacher conceded was "an outstanding manoeuvre".

THE HAMILTON EFFECT
2007

From the moment the 2007 Formula 1 season commenced at Australia's Albert Park circuit in Melbourne it was clear, even to those who display nothing more than a casual interest in the sport, that there was a true star in the ascendancy.

At just 22 years old, British driver Lewis Hamilton has taken motor racing's premier class by storm and embarrassed many seasoned campaigners in the process with a level of maturity that belies his years and an incredible grasp of race-craft that echoes the likes of Senna, Stewart and Schumacher. It is, therefore, no coincidence that Jackie Stewart himself has tipped the youngster to take the World Drivers' Championship title in his debut year or that Michael Schumacher has expressed surprise at his ability to consistently deliver results.

Hamilton was born in Stevenage, Hertfordshire, in January 1985 and experienced his first taste of motor sport racing his radio-controlled car at the age of five. Within a year he was so proficient at its controls that he appeared on BBC television's Blue Peter. Nobody could have guessed where that first interest in four-wheeled sport would take him. That year his father bought him his first go-kart and once more he took to it like a duck to water. After a couple of years he started racing and soon began to win on a regular basis.

At the age of 9 he was introduced to McLaren team principal Ron Dennis at which point he asked if he could race for the team in the future. Four years later their paths crossed again when Hamilton was signed to the McLaren driver development support programme becoming the youngest ever driver to secure a contract in Formula 1. Hamilton's karting career culminated in 2000 when he won the European Formula A Championship with maximum points and the Formula A World Cup.

Following his karting success a move to cars was inevitable. In 2003 he won the Formula Renault UK Championship for Manor Motorsports scoring an impressive 11 pole positions and 10 wins from 15 starts. In 2004 Hamilton moved to Formula 3 finishing fifth in the Championship before going on to take the title in 2005 at his second attempt. Next followed a move to the fiercely

competitive, 21 race GP2 Series. With five wins to his name he took the title at his first attempt once again bringing his exploits to the attention of Dennis.

To the amazement of the Formula 1 world he was signed to drive for Vodafone McLaren Mercedes for the 2007 season. This was a significant moment for the driver, the team and the sport as a whole. For Hamilton he was realising a life's ambition in taking his seat behind the controls of a Formula 1 racing car. For the team it was a big gamble – Hamilton was young and inexperienced and, it was argued, there were others who deserved the seat more. For the sport it was the first time a black driver had been seen in the Formula 1 paddock.

Hamilton did not disappoint. In his first race at Melbourne he stunned the world by qualifying in fourth place obscuring experienced drivers like Giancarlo Fisichella and Ralf Schumacher. But this achievement was soon eclipsed by his race performance where he finished third behind Ferrari's Kimi Räikkönen and his own team mate, reigning world champion Fernando Alonso. In doing so Hamilton became the first driver to finish on the podium in his debut race since Jacques Villeneuve in 1996.

Fantastic as this was, many assumed that this was just a flash in the pan moment for a precociously talented youngster. They were quickly proved wrong when three weeks later he went one better: qualifying in fourth once again but finishing second in the race behind Alonso. His form continued to Bahrain the following week where he qualified on the front row alongside pole-sitter Felipe Massa's Ferrari whilst his team mate was relegated to fourth behind Räikkönen.

At the fourth round of the championship, held on the Catalunya circuit in Spain, Hamilton again qualified in fourth position behind Massa, Alonso and Räikkönen. As the race got away on its second attempt (the first being aborted after Jarno Trulli stalled his Toyota on the grid) Alonso and Massa charged into the first corner but the warring pair touched sending the World Champion into the gravel. All of a sudden Hamilton found himself running in second place whist his team mate battled to make up for lost ground. Despite a fire in the pits almost putting an end to his race, Felipe Massa went on to take the win but Hamilton had valiantly held onto his position to take his third second-placed finish of the season and in doing so had become the youngest ever driver to lead the World Drivers' Championship. Further in the season he took his first ever victory at the Canadian Grand Prix, proving his credentials. Whether, as Frank Williams described him, he truly is superhuman remains to be seen. What is certain is that Lewis Hamilton is set to be one of the greatest Formula 1 drivers of all time.

ALSO AVAILABLE IN THIS SERIES

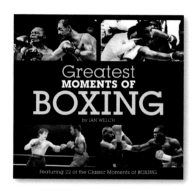

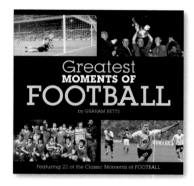

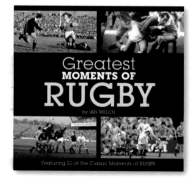

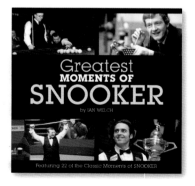

THE PICTURES IN THIS BOOK WERE PROVIDED COURTESY OF THE FOLLOWING:

GETTY IMAGES
101 Bayham Street, London NW1 0AG

LAT PHOTOGRAPHIC
www.latphoto.co.uk

Concept and Creative Direction:
VANESSA and KEVIN GARDNER

Design and Artwork: KEVIN GARDNER

Image research: ELLIE CHARLESTON

PUBLISHED BY GREEN UMBRELLA PUBLISHING

Publishers:
JULES GAMMOND and VANESSA GARDNER

Written by: JON STROUD